Follow Your Heart
Navigating a Terminal Diagnosis

By Gail Pope
President & Founder,
BrightHaven

Cover Art: Blanca Walker
Editing, Layout & Design: Carol Howe Hulse & Kate Fenton

Disclaimer

I am not a veterinarian or a therapist. The material contained in this booklet is not meant to be prescriptive in any way, shape or form for animals or humans.
I have, however, been helping our BrightHaven animals holistically since 1990, aided by many talented professional practitioners, and so I speak to you from our experiences along the way.

Always consult your veterinarian in matters concerning the health of your animals. *Any sign of pain in your animal should be immediately addressed with your veterinarian.*

Proceeds from the sale of this booklet will help BrightHaven to assist more senior, chronically ill and disabled animals.

To order more copies visit www.amazon.com. If you purchase via https://smile.amazon.com/ and select BrightHaven as your favorite charitable organization, Amazon will donate a percentage of the sale price to BrightHaven!

Follow Your Heart:
Navigating a Terminal Diagnosis

BrightHaven
44489 Town Center Way, Ste. D 487, Palm Desert, CA 92260
gail@brighthaven.org

Founded in 1990 by Gail and Richard Pope, nonprofit BrightHaven has evolved into a unique rescue, hospice and holistic education center focusing on senior, disabled and chronically ill animals, a vulnerable population that has an overwhelming need to find love and support in our society.

BrightHaven provides leadership in the development and application of animal hospice and its philosophy, which is modeled on human hospice. We are dedicated to improving the care and support for senior, special needs or chronically ill animals, most especially those approaching the end of life. We foster respect and awareness for animals as sentient beings and promote an understanding of death as a natural part of life.

Our mission is one of healing for body, mind and spirit for our animal family. We seek healing for their highest good rather than a cure and firmly believe that in order to have a "good death," one must prepare or set the stage for that to happen. I have written about that in my book, The BrightHaven Guide to Animal Hospice. Available at https://smile.amazon.com/.

At BrightHaven, when an animal enters hospice care our expectation is that the animal will have a painless, loving, peaceful journey followed by a painless, loving, peaceful and natural death. My booklet *Soar, My Butterfly: The Animal Dying Experience* was written to help caregivers understand the stages, signs and symptoms of the dying process. Available at https://smile.amazon. com/.

To learn more about BrightHaven, please visit www.brighthaven.org.

Additional BrightHaven Resources:
- Consultations with Gail Pope regarding BrightHaven's holistic and animal hospice care: Send an email to consultations@bright-haven.org.
- *The BrightHaven Guide to Animal Hospice* online learning program: www.brighthaven.org/education.
- *Walking With My Dog Through (End of) Life*: An intimate look at a profound life passage, written by BrightHaven's Education Program Specialist Carol Howe Hulse. Available at https://smile.amazon.com/.
- More resources are provided at the end of this booklet.

Wake-up Call

Distant song beckons.
Well-worn path recedes from view.
Change is in the air...

By Carol Howe Hulse.
BrightHaven Education Program Specialist

Dedication

This booklet is dedicated with love and appreciation:

- to all of the wonderful animals who helped me gather this knowledge by sharing their lives and deaths, and

- to Barbara Karnes RN, whose extremely helpful works about the human dying experience inspired me to share my knowledge by creating a BrightHaven series of booklets.

Table of Contents

Introduction

The Wake-Up Call

> Sometimes it takes a wake-up call, doesn't it,
> to alert us to the fact that we're hurrying through our lives
> instead of actually living them;
> that we're living the fast life instead of the good life?
> And I think, for many people, that wake-up call
> takes the form of an illness.
> ~Carl Honoré

Sometimes we are given a wake-up call by Mother Nature when we notice our beloved animal just being not quite themselves. We may see emotional or physical changes, indications of pain, perhaps a decline in appetite, some vomiting, diarrhea and changes in energy or behavior.

And so here we are at the vet's office having had an exam, some diagnostic work and an evaluation, after which we've received the news that this illness is likely not curable, which in fact means that death may be just around the corner. Here follows the time to take a deep breath and try to remain centered—something that is not easy for us to do when fear and panic are creeping in, and most especially when the life of one of our most beloved family members is threatened.

As sad and scary as this news is, it may also mean that we have been given precious time and how we choose to use that time is up to us. Many humans and animals are living with a life-threatening illness and have found balance and enjoyment in their daily lives with each new day being a priceless gift.

Countless distressed animal guardians have reached out to me for help after their animal has received a terminal diagnosis. They want to do what's best for their loved one, but they need help finding their way through the confusion and complexity of choices a terminal diagnosis can bring.

I wrote this little booklet to try to hold your hand and help you to navigate this path with a deeper sense of peace and clarity. It offers practical advice both for when you are at the vet's office as well as once home again with the family. It addresses important considerations and options as the way forward is planned and explores the possibility of hospice care and the natural dying process.

The booklet does not support any specific methodology or belief, but simply shares some guidelines from the BrightHaven perspective, to help you to make choices with awareness and with love. There's no one right approach or answer—it depends on many factors unique to each situation.

When Your Veterinarian Tells You There's Nothing More They Can Do...

This important topic comes up quite often in my consultations. Sometimes we just need someone to tell us that we already have the courage and ability we need to get through a difficult situation. This quote from a famous children's book is a useful reminder of that.

> Promise me you'll always remember:
> You're braver than you believe,
> and stronger than you seem,
> and smarter than you think.
> (Christopher Robin to Winnie-the-Pooh)
> ~*A. A. Milne*

End-of-life and hospice care are pretty much taken for granted in the world of human medicine and yet they are very much in their infancy in the veterinary world—often regardless of whether the veterinarian is conventional, holistic or even integrative. Education is very much needed!

I guess it is all about fear, and most humans are raised to fear death. There is no end-of-life education for children or young adults and so most people become very afraid of death. This is mostly (in my own opinion) why vets shy away from the time when they feel they have no more tools to offer a caregiver whose animal may be approaching the end of life—and that makes them wish to run in the opposite direction! When that happens, people are left anxious and worried and very often choose euthanasia as they feel they have no other option.

Interestingly, it is a true statement that if
we are not dead, then we are actually ALIVE,
and my focus is to care for the being for their entire journey
of being alive.
This is a very different approach than the focus of caring
for the dying...

Happily, there are many who share my own beliefs, and animal hospice care is slowly becoming more and more well known and recognized as a veterinary specialty. I hope that by sharing some of the individuals and organizations who may be able to help or offer direction for you that we can together spread the word to help others in the future who are faced with the same dilemma. Please visit the Resources section at the end of this booklet for more information.

Most of all, I encourage you to let your heart be your compass on this journey.

This seems to me to be a good time to share part of a Q and A session with Norman Cousins, who was an American political journalist, professor, author and world peace advocate, regarding his wonderful quotation: "Don`t deny the diagnosis, defy the verdict."

Question
What do you mean by "Don`t deny the diagnosis, defy the verdict"?

 I mean a serious illness can`t be dealt with by saying, "I really don`t have it."

What you have to do is say to yourself, "Yes, I do have this illness, but I`ll be darned if I`m going to accept the outcome that`s usually attached to it."

The reason for the defiance is that it opens up possibilities and enabling the   body to respond. I have seen literally hundreds of cases in which the patient refused to accept the prediction of his doctor—six months or a year to live—and then those predictions didn`t come true. Only God can give someone a year to live, not another human being.

Never stop dreaming,
never stop believing,
Change course, but don't give up.
Do not fear failure but rather, fear not trying.
and never stop learning.

~Roy T. Bennett, The Light in the Heart

Chapter 1: It's All About Love and Support, and It Starts with You!

As stated in Corinthians 13:13, "Three things will last forever—faith, hope and love—and the greatest of these is love."

This very difficult and challenging time IS all about living faith, embracing hope and sharing love. It seems to me these qualities are possibly our most important assets in the situation faced after a terminal diagnosis has been received. So we must begin with a little support for you, the caregiver.

To be faced with a terminal diagnosis, and sometimes accompanied by a recommendation for euthanasia, is perhaps the worst fear for anyone who deeply loves an animal companion.

Any decision should be made in, with, and for LOVE. It should not be made in haste or be driven by fear.

The power of love has long been an important part of Bright-Haven's Menu for Healing and the profound healing effects of love simply cannot be overstated. (For the full menu, please see page 23.) We know that when we are in a state of love and compassion our energy changes and radiates out into the world, affecting others whether we're aware of it or not. We know that insufficient love is the root cause of dis-ease as it makes people sick, both directly and indirectly. We also know that the power of love can transform an ordinary moment into a magical one. It reminds us of alchemy, the medieval chemical science seeking, amongst other things, to discover a way of indefinitely prolonging life.

"

The BrightHaven animals live well before and during hospice care, which will help you to better understand how they die gently and peacefully. Our philosophy is quite simple and is all about achieving a balance of healing for body, mind and spirit. It embraces living in the moment in love and joy and the understanding that healing, which is primarily influenced by love, compassion and balance, is required for both living and dying. At this point we cannot know what the journey that lies ahead will bring, but we can focus on offering love accompanied by healing for the highest good for the animal.

This is the time to take several deep breaths, become more centered and well balanced and understand that in order to be both loving and supportive, you must be strong. This is also the time for self-care to become a priority. One powerful reminder is the air mask analogy—put your own mask on first. You have to take care of yourself, so you can be present for your animal.

You are doing your best to care for and support this precious being, and that is all you can do.

The above sentence is very important, and I emphasize that guilt has no place here. It is important that you try to eradicate it from daily life. You are indeed doing your best and that is all you can do. Your beloved animal will know this and be comforted by that knowledge. Do not beat yourself up about anything. Let go of guilt and self-doubt and move forward in the love you and your animal share.

> It is the energy behind the method that heals.
> In our culture we tend to be addicted to methods, forgetting
> that ultimately it is being a vessel of love that is the
> greatest form of healing.
> ~*Sandra Ingerman*

Supportive Tips
-     Understand and support yourself so you can be there to

support your animal friend.
- Reassure yourself you're doing the best you can.
- Be willing to reach out for help.
- Let go of fear and guilt.
- Do what you can and then let go.
- Remember panic is not a helpful energy.
- Understand that dying is a process, and you have time to think.
- Realize that your initial choices may change along the way as your animal's condition or situation evolves, and as you gather additional information.
- When contemplating a decision, put yourself in your animal's position and think what you would want.
- Meditate, even for just a few minutes, to enhance your wellbeing.

> Mindfulness is like that—
> it is the miracle which can call back in a flash
> our dispersed mind and restore it to wholeness
> so that we can live each minute of life.
> *~Thich Nhat Hanh*

More Thoughts for the Caregiver

As one considers the future and what it may bring, it can be very helpful to realize that not only might our perspective on living and dying need to change; we might be in for some other surprises as well, such as recovery and renewed health. Later in this booklet we will visit animal hospice care, which may be appropriate for some, and it is important to consider that many terminally ill human patients enter hospice care only to discover a new balance for the physical and emotional, leading to renewed, healthier and longer life.

We have become a disposable society with electronics thrown away instead of being repaired, as are cars, appliances, clothes, and often animals past the age of twelve! As we grow, we learn about life and the birthing process as a matter of course but are taught virtually nothing about the end-of-life process, and so death has become a difficult concept at best and one to be feared by most. Death remains the big fear for most people, not only their own, but the fear of witnessing the death of others. So, when they have a choice to avoid dealing with it, they often do and thus the principal way for an animal to die is by euthanasia.

In other words, looking at both ends of life, we believe that death is a process as is birth, and as we would not advocate C-section for all births, nor would we advocate euthanasia for all deaths.

Animals live in the moment and appear to show no fear of illness or death, and to be present together with them during the last chapter of life is a deeply rewarding and valuable experience. It often challenges old ways of thinking, reveals our deepest neediness and plummets us into uncertainty. At the same time, it is an opportunity for growth and discovery, a journey requiring courage and flexibility and enabling us to cultivate a wiser heart, deeper compassion and an increased capacity for skillful action.

As in birth, where midwives are needed to offer love, company, soothing treatments and words of comfort and support, so they are also required at the other end of life. It is the same revolving doorway, perhaps, with some coming in and others going out...

The BrightHaven Menu for Self-Care
As we have developed our Menu for Healing, we have also created a similar menu as a guide for successful self-care, which is so very important in the often long and winding road ahead. As in our healing menu we emphasize love as the first and last item but this time it is self-love. Here is our Menu for Self-Care:

- Love yourself unreservedly.
- Have faith in the greater plan. Everything will work out just as it's meant to.
- Accept what IS in your heart.
- Be grateful—each and every new day is a gift.
- Show kindness to yourself as well as others.
- Try not to be judgmental of yourself or of others.
- Believe in healing for the highest good.
- Watch your breath and live for the moment.
- Be open to change.
- Smile—it's healing and contagious!
- And again, love yourself unreservedly.

Let us next look at practical considerations while at the veterinarian's office…

Chapter 2: At the Vet's Office: The Practicalities

Faith and hope work hand in hand,
however, while hope focuses on the future,
faith focuses on the now.

~David Odunaiya

This chapter is written as a helpful guide for when you are at the veterinarian's office before, during or after receiving a terminal diagnosis.

Here you are, pressed for time, perhaps, and certainly feeling stressed. You are facing uncertainty and the worry that comes along with it, and the more you know, the better choices you can make and the lower the fear will become.

This section gives the basic and most important questions that need immediate answers in order to make a quick decision for or against euthanasia, or for taking your loved one home. What care is needed to maintain life in order for me/us to think things through?

Be sure that your veterinarian understands that you are not dis-respecting or rejecting his advice; you are simply wishing to take a little time to discuss the situation with the family and to be sure you are making the right choice for everyone. Ideally you do not want to make this decision in the midst of an emotionally charged moment. It's important to realize too that some vets may gently push euthanasia for a variety of reasons, including their own, very human fears surrounding dying and death.

Discussion Guidance
Here are some suggestions for your discussion with your veterinarian:
- Take a deep breath!
- Ask the vet for the diagnosis and a clear explanation of it.
- Remember: It is the vet's responsibility to share a realistic prognosis and discuss anticipated outcomes with the family.

o   What are the odds of accomplishing a cure?
•	Be sure you understand all the information and ask for explanations.
•	Do not allow yourself to be frightened by medical terminology.
•	Find out as much as you can about your animal's condition and what options may be available.
•	Request that the medical notes be forwarded to you.
•	Ask about surgery, a second opinion or specialist assessment, if applicable.
•	Ask what drugs may be prescribed and their possible side effects.
•	Consider and discuss holistic, conventional or integrative healthcare options
•	Ask if hospice and palliative care would be appropriate and find out what that means and would entail.
•	Do not make hasty decisions if at all possible (in acute situations, sometimes a decision needs to be made on the spot).
•	Understand if care can be managed at home; if not, have the vet explain why not.
o   Is oxygen necessary?
o   What about pain medications/other drugs?
•	Discuss costs for new treatment protocols, at-home hospice care or euthanasia.
•	Consider seeking advice and support from an animal hospice professional.

In other words:
Consider taking your animal home to give everyone time to make a fully informed decision as to care, treatment, hospice care, natural death or euthanasia unless your animal is in an acute situation.

Should you decide you wish to take your animal home with you, then there are more questions to be asked related to medical care:
•	Ask what medications are recommended to go home with you.
•	Find out what they do and if they may have side effects

- Understand what the daily care regimen would entail.
- Ask if current symptoms will be likely to multiply or intensify.
- Understand what new symptoms are likely to be encountered.
- Find out if pain is present now or expected as a part of the medical condition.
    - o Ask how it should be treated.
    - o An important note is that pain usually does not appear suddenly at the end-of-life if it has not been a part of the animal's ongoing illness.
- Ask for information and options for holistic, conventional or integrative treatment. BrightHaven uses primarily holistic care but turns to conventional drugs if and when necessary, making integrative care well worth consideration—that way taking the best from both worlds! This will be explained in more detail a little later in this chapter.
- Ask about hospice and palliative care, comfort and end-of-life care and what type of support your vet offers and/or can refer.
- Discuss treatment protocol costs for at-home care and also euthanasia, as financial considerations factor into the decision process.

Points for Consideration
- The veterinarian is trained to do everything possible to save the life.
- If a veterinarian says "I can do no more," it is very often after they have pulled out all the stops to fight manifesting symptoms.
- It's important to step back and consider the patient. For example, evaluate palliative/comfort/hospice care versus continuing intervention. What would the patient want?
- Sometimes palliative/comfort/hospice care may be the better way to go.

These ARE a lot of questions to ask and if your veterinarian seems unwilling or unable to gather all the information requested, then you may want to consider finding another veterinarian to assist you.

Remember, too, that, after due consideration it is for the family to make decisions based upon what they have learned and what their hearts tell them.

Care Choices
Many people do not quite understand the differences in care choices, so here are the basics:

Palliative or Comfort Care
The goal of palliative care is achievement of the best quality of life for patients and their families. It's not the same as hospice as it doesn't only serve the dying. Instead, palliative care focuses on improving life and providing comfort at different stages of life involving serious, chronic or life-threatening illnesses.

Other characteristics:

•	The focus is to bring comfort and relief from symptoms and the stress of an illness.
•	It may be started at any stage of an illness.
•	Palliative/comfort care has no curative intent.
•	A multidisciplinary or team approach is effective.
•	Specialized medical care is utilized.
•	Care is focused on the patient's and family's needs.
•	Emotional and spiritual concerns are addressed.
•	Palliative care can go on as long as it is needed, for months and even for years.

Hospice Care (includes palliative care)
Hospice care involves a team approach, existing to provide support and care for patients in the last phases of incurable disease, or at the natural end of life. Hospice incorporates all of palliative care; and is defined as a philosophy, a specialized program of care, and in some instances, an actual place for the dying.

Other characteristics:
•	Hospice care begins when death is perceived to be the

eventual outcome and when the goal shifts from cure to comfort.
•   The goal is comfort and for life to be lived as fully as possible until the time of death.
•   A natural death is typically the assumed goal of hospice care.
•   Care is focused on the patient's and family's needs.
•   Emotional and spiritual concerns are addressed.
•   The focus is intensive caring instead of intensive care.
•   Care neither prolongs nor hastens death.
•   Hospice care aims to provide a degree of preparation for death.
•   Hospice care recognizes that dying is a normal process, whether or not resulting from disease.
•   Death is viewed as a natural part of life, not a failed medical event to be feared or avoided.
•   The end-of-life period is viewed as an opportunity for growth.

Hospice Care Versus End-of-Life Care Versus Palliative/Comfort Care
The main difference between hospice care and end-of-life care is that hospice care does not foresee euthanasia in the future but focuses on a peaceful and gentle, natural death. After all, life itself is terminal.

Of course, it's quite permissible for an animal in hospice care to take a turn for the worse and the decision to euthanize be made, whereas in palliative or end-of-life care euthanasia may be the expected outcome.

Remember, too, that it is also possible for an animal in any of these types of care to take a turn for the better. BrightHaven finds this to be the case repeatedly when utilizing holistic methods. Most often BrightHaven animals approaching the end-of-life experience peaks and valleys in their health and enjoy times when we wonder what lies ahead...

Many times what does lie ahead is a period of renewed energy and feeling of wellbeing, and we have learned to enjoy and celebrate these days or weeks and sometimes months without question or worry about when life will end.

Whatever path for comfort care you choose, there is also the option to care for your animal holistically, conventionally or integratively.

Some Helpful Definitions
Conventional Medicine
Conventional medicine is what you get from medical doctors, nurses, physical therapists, psychologists, and similar health care professionals.

You might hear it called: Standard medical care, biomedicine, allopathic medicine, Western medicine, mainstream medicine, orthodox medicine.

Reference: www.webmd.com/cancer/qa/what-is-conventional-medicine

Holistic Medicine
Holistic medicine is a form of healing that considers the whole person—body, mind, spirit, and emotions—in the quest for optimal health and wellness.
According to the holistic medicine philosophy, one can achieve optimal health—the primary goal of holistic medicine practice—by gaining proper balance in life.

Holistic medicine practitioners believe that the whole person is made up of interdependent parts and if one part is not working properly, all the other parts will be affected. In this way, if people have imbalances (physical, emotional or spiritual) in their lives, it can negatively affect their overall health.

Reference: www.webmd.com/balance/guide/what-is-holistic-medicine#1

Integrative medicine pairs traditional medicine with other treatments to care for your mind, body and spirit. For example, your doctor may suggest chemotherapy to fight cancer as well as acupuncture to help manage its side effects.

It isn't just medicine. Your care team may also design a plan to help you build healthy behaviors and skills—like smart eating habits and stress-busting activities. These things can keep you healthy for the long term.

Integrative medicine uses complementary treatments, but they have to be backed by good science.

Reference: www.webmd.com/cancer/holistic-treatment-17/integrative-medicine

Understand that your choices will be part of an ongoing process:

- **Your animal's condition/situation will most likely change.**
- **As you gather more information and continually check in with yourself and your animal, priorities and decision factors may change.**

The BrightHaven Way

During my journey into the world of holistic medicine, I have been privileged to witness amazing returns to better health and longevity for many animals, experiencing a profound mind shift about healing and wellness as a result.

From our perspective, there's a difference between curing and healing. Curing is typically thought of as achieving the absence of disease and it is what medical science attempts to do through medication, treatment and other forms of external intervention.

Healing is an internal process. It is all about restoring the balance and harmony of the body, mind and spirit and is essential when the adverse influences of loss, illness or life changes have affected one's life. Most importantly, healing can be achieved without a cure.

The animals have taught that for some, healing will bring about new and wonderful life. For others, healing is necessary to prepare for death and the beyond.

The BrightHaven Menu for Healing
It is also our firm belief that one's quality of life will very much influence the quality of one's dying process and so the BrightHaven Menu for Healing, introduced briefly in Chapter 1, always focuses on the best quality of life all the way to the most peaceful and loving dying process.

Here is our Menu for Healing, affectionately called "The Love Sandwich," since it begins and ends with love:

- Love.
- Diet—raw meat based, fully supplemented.
- Diagnostics.
- Classical veterinary homeopathy for care at all life stages.
- Alternative vaccination protocol/titers.
- Immune and organ support, Reiki and other complementary therapies.
- Intuition.
- Natural path to death.
- Love.

For more details about our Menu for Healing, please visit our website: www.brighthaven.org/animal-wellbeing-menu-healing/

As mentioned at the beginning of this booklet and as stated in Corinthians 13:13, "Three things will last forever—faith, hope and love—and the greatest of these is love." These qualities may be our most important assets in the situation faced after a terminal diagnosis has been given. The first time I was told that love is the greatest healer I was somewhat skeptical. It just sounded too simple to be true, but as time has marched on I have seen the results for myself and it really makes good sense.

> Our sorrows and wounds are healed only
> when we touch them with compassion.
> *~Buddha*

Some ways that love heals:
- Love creates relaxation, which offers a space for healing.
- Love decreases anxiety and stress, which in time damage physical and mental health.
- Love sends our cells the message to repair and rejuvenate.
- Love helps us to feel better about ourselves, which leads to better self-care.
- Love causes the release of oxytocin, known as the feel-good or love hormone.
- Love also causes production of norepinephrine and dopamine in the brain, which promote feelings of joy and pleasure.
- Love decreases inflammation and improves the immune system.
- Sleeping next to someone you love brings relaxation.
- Dis-ease signifies disharmony in one's thoughts; love restores inner harmony

The BrightHaven Healing Path and Hospice Care
And so, the BrightHaven healing path can best be summed up by saying:

- We accept that not everything can be fixed.
- We use symptoms as our guides.
- Healing for the highest good is our motto.
- Energy healing is our way.
- We strongly support natural living and natural dying.
- We turn to conventional drugs if nothing else works.

BrightHaven hospice care is very much aligned with hospice care for humans, where love, comfort, dignity, quality of life and also quality for dying are of the highest importance, and the spiritual aspect of the journey is highly honored. We are privileged to have provided hospice care for and shared the dying experience with over 600 animals, who taught us so much about living and dying well.

BrightHaven animals have often come to us after a terminal diagnosis and many have lived longer and healthier lives than expected. Some have not, of course, and we have learned to follow our hearts and beliefs in the knowledge that we are doing our best, with love, and can do no more. This is very often the time when miracles can occur.

There are only two ways to live your life.
One is as though nothing is a miracle.
The other is as though everything is a miracle.

~Albert Einstein

Chapter 3: Planning the Way Forward

> Yesterday is but a dream,
> Tomorrow is only a vision.
> But today well lived makes every yesterday a dream
> of happiness,and every tomorrow a vision of hope.
> *~Kālidāsa, The Complete works of Kālidāsa*

Let's assume that you have returned home and are ready to start absorbing the news, reviewing the situation and digesting all the answers to your many questions for the vet. It's important to mention again that a terminal diagnosis most often does not mean that death is imminent and sometimes, with a change to healthcare and lifestyle, life can be prolonged.

Now seems to be a good time for a reminder of the wonderful quotation from Norman Cousins that I shared earlier: "Don`t deny the diagnosis, defy the verdict." A focus on the possibilities for healing is, in my opinion, one of your most powerful assets.

Determining Options
In order to determine options for healthcare, what will be involved and how it will impact the family, the following issues should be carefully discussed:

•	Pain and suffering–are they present? Can they be man-aged?
•	Quality of life for living–can it be improved and if so, how?
•	Quality of life for dying–what is that and how can it be achieved?
•	Will to live–how strong is it?
•	And very importantly, whether a natural dying process is desired, or euthanasia will be the goal.

Since pain, suffering, quality of life—or, possibly, quality of life for dying—and will to live are uppermost in the mind, we must begin with these issues.

I just love the simplicity of the quote below from The Hayagriva Buddhist Center for a topic that has such a broad reach into everyone's lives...and deaths:

Physical pain is a physiological process.
Mental pain comes from an agitated and disturbed mind.
Suffering is our mental and emotional response to the pain.
~Hayagriva Buddhist Center, www.hayagriva.org.au

Medical intuitive Catherine Carrigan sums up the differences in similar terms:
Pain is the physical experience.
It's an ache in your muscles, the strain in your joints, the fever and chills, the throbbing in your temples, the congestion in your sinuses, the stabbing in your upper back, the shooting sharpness down your leg.

Suffering is your emotional experience.
Suffering may or may not be connected to physical pain.
You can suffer emotionally even on a sunny day when nothing apparently bad is happening to you on the outside.
Suffering is the negative story you are telling yourself about what is happening now, what has happened in the past or what could potentially happen in the future.

Clearly pain and suffering are so closely linked as to almost be inseparable. Maybe our best route is to learn as much as we possibly can about pain, and hope that in turn we will be able to minimize the ensuing suffering we or our animal may feel.

Here are some questions and answers regarding pain for guidance:
- How can pain be identified?
    o Animals sometimes do not show pain, and so the first priority is to identify its presence and degree as accurately as possible. Some signs might be: changes in behavior, personality or appetite; reactivity to touch in affected areas; dilated pupils and

physiologic changes.

- How can the level of pain be determined?
	o Perhaps the best way to evaluate pain levels is to look at the symptom as expressed. For example, some expressions of these changes could be: the inability to jump or walk well, limping, lethargy, hiding, panting; also, open-mouthed breathing, vocalizing, screaming, restlessness, discomfort.
- Are these the aches and pains of old age, or do they need addressing?
	o It is always good to consult a veterinarian for advice. Sometimes a change in diet, or treatment by homeopathy or acupuncture or other form of holistic medicine, can make a world of difference.
- What are options to address pain?
	o Drugs, homeopathy, acupuncture, herbs, TCM (Traditional Chinese Medicine), cannabis, Reiki, essential oils/aromatherapy, biofeedback, chiropractic, massage, vitamins, supplements and more.
- Does untreated pain affect the quality of life?
	o Yes, it does, and that is why we must become proactive.
- Does pain always need managing?
	o Good question! Ask the animal. Very often it may not need managing and will be temporary. Drugs are sometimes prescribed due to the fear of pain by the human, without considering the wisdom of Mother Nature. We have often contemplated the use of a drug, but by the time we have it prescribed, the animal is no longer evincing the need.
- Is there ever a downside to administering drugs?
	o Once drugs are given they are very often continued, as no one knows when, if or how to stop, as pain is assumed. The suppression of symptoms may not always be the best thing. One must eventually die of "something," and when symptoms are heavily suppressed, other more serious physical or mental issues may be triggered, rather than allowing for the natural progression of the body to its demise.
- Is the process of dying painful?
	o Human hospice teaches us dying itself is NOT painful

and that—IMPORTANTLY—if pain has not been present during chronic illness then it will not appear in death. My own mother told me repeatedly that she was experiencing no pain during her dying process.

- Does the presence of pain warrant euthanasia?
  o I believe that if strong pain cannot be controlled, then yes, euthanasia may be appropriate, and should be based upon the facts and the animal and not the person's own discomfort or pain.
- If there is pain at death, do you think the pain is similar to that of birth?
  o It may be. Pain always seems present during birth, although at various levels. Many people accept pain control and others choose to follow and endure the natural path. Perhaps it may be somewhat similar during the process of dying, although we know that dying itself is not painful and so any pain manifesting may stem from a chronic illness.
- Humans faint sometimes when experiencing acute pain. Can animals do the same thing?
  o Mother Nature provided this as an escape for pain and yes, animals and humans can "step out" or away from their physical bodies if needed. Possibly they return when the physical self is more comfortable.
- How can you help?
  o Remain calm and soothing. Do not panic. Show love and call your veterinarian for help and guidance. Better still—be proactive and have strong, fast-acting medicine available before pain manifests.
- How do you deal with your own emotional pain?
  o Focus on living in the moment.

Here is perhaps the most important question:
- Will your veterinarian supply pain meds for you to have on hand at home if needed?
  o If your veterinarian is supportive of you caring for your animal at home, then it is important that in case of need you have strong, fast-acting pain meds on hand that do not require swallowing.

Find a place (inside) where there's joy, and the joy will
burn out the pain.

~Joseph Campbell

- Pain is a symptom which can most often be treated very successfully.
- Modern day medicine has made great advances in recent times in the area of pain control, and much can be done to relieve signs of pain, which in turn equates to suffering in many minds.
- A spiritual understanding of suffering is invaluable when discussing quality of life in the context of animal hospice. The physical body, be it human or animal, is only a temporary vehicle to be occupied during our short time on earth.

Simply put, pain is and should be a part of life and does not necessarily equate to suffering in all cases. When we see symptoms of pain in our residents, we are most often able to effectively treat with homeopathy, animal Reiki, other alternative therapies or conventional drugs depending on the needs of the animal. There is much fear and often anger surrounding the questions that arise around the topic of suffering, and it may be good, therefore, to have a focus based on achieving a state of wellness, joy or balance whether for continued life or for transition.

BrightHaven's goal is for the animal to live well through their last breath. After reviewing the above considerations, here are two important criteria:

- At what level are they suffering and how or can that be alleviated?
- At what level are you suffering and how and can that be alleviated?

We shall draw from the heart of suffering itself the means
of inspiration and survival.

~Winston Churchill

In order to evaluate these two questions, we need to address quality of life both for living and also for the dying process.

Quality of Life for Living (or Dying)

Health-related quality of life (HRQoL) is a multi-dimensional concept that includes domains related to physical, mental, emotional,
and social functioning. It goes beyond direct measures of population
health, life expectancy, and causes of death, and focuses on the
impact health status has on quality of life. A related concept of
HRQoL is well-being, which assesses the positive aspects of a
person's life, such as positive emotions and life satisfaction.

Reference: www.healthypeople.gov/2020/about/foundation-
health-measures/Health-Related-Quality-of-Life-and-Well-Being

In human hospice care, one does one's absolute best to make
quality of the life be the very finest it can be, by whatever means
available, and one never gives up or stops trying. In the world of
animals, we have been given the powerful privilege of euthanasia
to use if we, the guardians, see no other possible alternative. At
BrightHaven we consider euthanasia to be our last resort. Perhaps, then, the basic interpretation of quality of life revolves
around the discussion of natural dying and euthanasia.

It seems that often, as they try to decide upon whether to euthanize, people become focused on quality of life. BrightHaven's focus is simply a day-by-day mission to bring joy and healing to help
the animal live as fully as possible. Therein lies the difference, as
in the early years of BrightHaven, many animals were euthanized
as we, or our veterinarians, determined "it was time" to end their
suffering. Our vision and views have vastly changed since those
days as we have reached a greater understanding of the circle of
life, death and beyond.
BrightHaven places great emphasis not only on quality of life, but
also on quality of dying or death. Much has been penned on this
controversial subject. A scale for better understanding of how to
measure the quality of life has been developed by Alice Villalo-
bos, DVM, DPNAP. The scale comprises a list, called "HHHHHMM",

which stands for hurt, hunger, hydration, hygiene, happiness, mobility, and more good days than bad days. A score above 5 on most of these issues is acceptable in maintaining an end-of-life program. Dr. Alice very rightly says, too, that each pet's situation needs an individual, kind and supportive approach.

While following a scale can be tremendously helpful in your understanding, you are urged to add another "H" to that list—that of "heart"—and following your own! It may well be time to consider euthanasia, but it may also be a time to become proactive. Many veterinarians are not educated in the options for animal hospice care, as well as how to support the dying process with regard to pain management and quality of life. You are urged to pause to explore the possibilities for an alternative route for care.

Poor quality of life does not necessarily translate to "I want to die." Life is precious, and we all try to keep it for ourselves as long as possible. We know the will for survival is huge. To our thinking at BrightHaven, this is an area where the worlds of animal and human hospice could better align. When our animals' quality of life does not match our wish for them it is often hard for humans to bear; however, perhaps one should try to think beyond one's own discomfort. Many older humans, and often younger ones too, may not have what we would deem a good or great quality of daily life, and yet we do not euthanize them—we simply seek to bring them more pleasure, and very often can and do. Some actively express their own joy and bring it to the world.
We have often heard said the words, "How can you see them lying there suffering, day after day?" Very frequently our answer is, "Are you sure of their suffering—or is it yours?" Very often suffering proves to be in the eye of the beholder and based in their deep-rooted fear of death.

The quality of life depends on the power of love
and quality and quantity of happiness.
~Debasish Mridha

Introducing "The PEACEFUL Checklist"

Quality of life is a familiar discussion to most of us, but the conversation surrounding the achievement of a suitable quality of life for the process of dying is new. There is a great difference between quality of life for living and quality of life for the dying process.

BrightHaven is proud to have joined forces with Spirits in Transition (www.spiritsintransition.org) and The Nikki Hospice Foundation for Pets (www.pethospice.org) to create GRACE (Gratitude and Respect for Animals and their Care at End-of-life), a consortium devoted to animal hospice care.

I am pleased to present the GRACE PEACEFUL checklist. It has been designed for use in hospice-supported natural dying to determine acceptable quality of life to continue the normal dying process or to make the decision for euthanasia.

Hospice care is skilled comfort care to the end of a life wherein death is neither hastened nor postponed. In those exceptions when patient comfort cannot be adequately maintained, or the caregiver's emotional, physical, financial or other resources are insufficient, animal hospice care can be ended by euthanasia.

The PEACEFUL Checklist:
Pain, Emaciation, Appetite, Comfort, Eleventh Hour, Fluid, Unaware, Lethargy

Symptom	The Dying Process
Pain	Dying does not cause pain; disease causes pain. Adequate pain control is most important. Strong, fast acting, ideally sublingual pain medication is to be kept on hand in case of sudden need. If the disease process is prone to create, or has already caused, a need for oxygen supplementation, oxygen for home use must be kept on hand.
Emaciation	Substantial loss of body weight is normal at the end of life and generally does not constitute discomfort to the patient.
Appetite & Thirst	Decreasing appetite is normal during the dying process. It often precedes a loss of thirst. Neither is to be confused with reversible symptoms of a treatable condition. Consult with your hospice-trained veterinarian. For the dying body digestion is no longer a priority. Food should be offered, including by finger or syringe, until rejected; same with water. Complete disinterest is to be accepted. Giving food in the absence of hunger can cause considerable discomfort.
Comfort	Patient's environment should be kept clean, quiet and stress free. Anti-anxiety medicine should be kept on hand. It is essential that the caregiver remain as calm and present as possible. Comfort and dignity should be maintained via basic hygiene during the process of dying; *i.e.*, clean-up of urine, feces and other discharges.

Symptom	The Dying Process
Eleventh Hour—what else may be going on with the animal?	Eyes glassy or dull. Extremities cooler. Incontinence of bladder and/or bowels. Irregular breathing is normal. Congestion is normal but keep nostrils clean. Lips, gums and anus may be pale. To do: Keep environment quiet.
Fluid	Dehydration progresses; endorphins are released by the brain to promote comfort. The mouth can be kept moistened by drops of water only from a syringe, dropper or moistened applicator. Subcutaneous fluids may be helpful to a certain point along the process—consult with your hospice-trained veterinarian.
Unaware	For many animals, interest in the immediate environment dwindles at the end of life, as focus turns inward. Some animals may remain responsive and a little interactive until late stages. Restlessness may occur as the animal experiences normal changes occurring in his/her body. Severe agitation must be addressed—consult with your hospice-trained veterinarian.
Low energy, listlessness	As life energy dwindles, most animals will be recumbent at the end of life, resting peacefully the majority of the time.

This checklist is available for download at www.brighthaven.org/quality-dying-checklist/.

To combat death, you don't need much of a life, just one
that isn't yet finished.
~*Herta Müller,* The Hunger Angel: A Novel

Will to Live

The will to live is a psychological force to fight for survival seen
as an important and active process of conscious and unconscious
reasoning. This occurs particularly when one's own life
is threatened by a serious injury or disease.
~*Wikipedia,* www.wikipedia.org

The will to live seems to be the strongest of feelings. People and animals approaching death often demonstrate a huge push for survival. Everyone suffers at one level or another, so it is a difficult conversation when held at a time close to the end of life. Things can appear uncomfortable or difficult, particularly if the being becomes immobilized in some way. Remember that loss of mobility, which many may perceive as suffering, is a very normal part of the dying process.

However, when that human sits up later and perhaps smiles, enjoys a little conversation, possibly takes a sip or two of water—or an animal wags a feeble tail, savors a chin rub, maybe purrs happily or enjoys a cuddle and a lick of your face—these are moments to treasure.

Many times, humans or animals will indeed be seen as suffering at any stage of their life, but if they have the will to live and can find some joy in their day…,

I had seen these transformations, people who had lost
their will to live, coming back from their zombie states
and radiating a new life force from their eyes.
~*Anthony Kiedis,* Scar Tissue

Chapter 4: At Home and Making Your Decisions

> May the sun bring you new energy by day,
> May the moon softly restore you by night,
> May the rain wash away your worries.
> May the breeze blow new strength into your being.
> May you walk gently through the world and know
> its beauty all the days of your life.
>
> *~Apache blessing*

You have a lot of information to consider, and once in the privacy of your own home it is time to review and digest it all, to decide what to accept and what to reject. A good place to begin is in contemplation of your animal's current quality of life. Can it be improved and if so, how? Would some changes to diet, healthcare and lifestyle be appropriate and actionable?

Here are some practical considerations:

- Can care be managed at home?
- Which path appeals most—holistic, conventional or integrative health care?
- Could a change to diet help,,maybe raw meat-based or organic canned?
  - o Consider the addition of immune and organ support.
- What other items might improve quality of life?
  - o Mobility aids for traction or a wheelchair or incontinence wear.
  - o A new bed.
  - o Exercise.
- Are there options for respite care assistance?
- What'll friends and neighbors think?
  - o And that question leads me to introduce The Animal Hospice Care Certificate.

The Animal Hospice Care Certificate

Let's consider daily life and what that will look like. Do you perchance have an animal with an obvious tumor, or an emaciated dog or cat in the garden or out on a walk that will attract questions or concern from friends, neighbors or passersby?

The last thing anyone would wish for is that some well-meaning person calls animal control or other authority to report an animal appearing to need care and attention. So it's wise to have paperwork on hand that is signed by your veterinarian and describes the situation and the fact that the animal is in hospice care at home under the supervision of a licensed veterinarian.

The Animal Hospice Certificate is available for download at www.brighthaven.org/animal-hospice-care-certificate/.
It should be displayed in an appropriate place or presented to anyone showing concern for what may appear to be an animal in need of veterinary care.

Discussions with Family and Friends
- Consider all options carefully with family and friends.
- Be open and honest with each other.
- Is the animal strong enough for any recommended treatment or protocol?
- If so, would that feel like an appropriate course of action?
- Consider will to live—is your animal ready to die?
- Talk with your animal too!
- Consider consulting a trusted animal telepath and medical intuitive. You will find our recommendation in the Suggested Resources section at the end of this booklet.
   o Please note: Sometimes an animal says it is time to let them go. You may wish to stop to consider whether they are requesting euthanasia or suggesting it is time for their loved one to let them go emotionally and accept that they are dying.
- Stay away from unsupportive people.
- Consider hospice or supportive care, what will be involved and how it will impact the family.
- Consider making an appointment with a professional animal hospice practitioner for a more informed discussion.

- Consider your own grief and feelings of guilt.
- Sleep on it if possible.
- Consider what is most appropriate for the animal and the family situation, including financially.
- Discover who feels that euthanasia is appropriate at this stage and who may wish to take things day by day to see how the future unfolds for the animal and the family.
- Understand that if natural death is desired that hospice care is a process, as are dying and also death, and there will be changes and choices to be made along the way.
- Be sure you understand the commitment needed to support a natural dying process.
- Above all, listen to and trust your intuition and follow your heart.

Making Your Decision
Life is eternal, and love is immortal, and death is only
a horizon; and a horizon is nothing save the limit of our sight.
~Rossiter Worthington Raymond

A Helpful Reminder
- The 50/50 rule:
  o 50% is what you do to help the animal to live well and be strong for journey through life and death.
  o 50% is taking care of YOU and supporting yourself while you walk with your loved one on his or her journey.

Only your compassion and your loving kindness are
invincible, and without limit.
~*Thich Nhat Hanh*

Offering More Practical Thoughts, Considerations or Options
a.	Hospice, End-of-life or Palliative Care
Finances:
- Given your living arrangements, work schedules and financial situation, is it viable to support palliative/hospice/end-of-life care and a natural death or euthanasia at home?

• If you have insurance, what will it cover?

Veterinary care:
• Will you require professional guidance and who will be your choice? A local animal hospice professional, email or telephone consultations with a classical veterinary homeopath, alongside assistance from your local veterinarian?
• Can your veterinarian offer support if needed and is s/he available 24/7?
• Does your vet offer a comfort kit to have on hand should the need arise, and does it contain a strong, fast-acting pain medicine that does not require swallowing?
    o   A comfort kit might contain items such as current medications including strong pain meds that may be needed, various sized syringes, homeopathic remedies, wound care or dressing items, eye drops, Rescue Remedy, a couple of jars of baby food, sponge applicators to moisten the mouth tissue, and more.

Daily care:
• What kind of care will be involved?
• Can you cope on your own at home or will help be needed, and does it need to be the team effort of hospice care?
• What might you need help with?
• Are you willing and/or able, or is it your wish, to implement some changes, perhaps for diet, healthcare, bedding, mobility aids and so on?
• What about around-the-clock care—is it required at this time and if so, can that be managed?
• Do you have supportive friends, family or neighbors to help with errands or respite care? It's important to surround yourself with supportive people.

A few more notes:
• You won't be available for your animal if you're occupied by trying to figure everything out at once.
• You don't need to go out and get and do everything at once.

- What feels like the best first step? Often a diet change is a good choice.
- It's a process—everything unfolds exactly as it's meant to.
- Bear in mind that your care and health plan will offer healing for the highest good of your beloved one in order they remain as comfortable, healthy and happy as possible during their journey. It will not be focused on cure per se, but do remain open for miracles…

b.   Natural Dying

- Consider that your role is to love and support your animal through the remainder of life and the dying process. You are helping them to give birth to a new life.
- A sick animal doesn't need anything that will cause the body more stress (flea & tick or heartworm meds, vaccines, etc.).
- No matter what you do, feed, try, say, think, etc., you can't control the dying process or when a being dies, but you can make it the best it can possibly be.
- God and the being determine the number of days…
- Life is impermanent, and from the moment of birth we may die at any time, whether we are young or old.
- It's all about the circle of life.
- Accept that when the animal wants to let go, it's time. Your animal's earthly mission is complete.
- What are your beliefs? Is there something beyond death? Knowing, and understanding your beliefs, can be very helpful. We at BrightHaven have had experiences that seem to confirm there is indeed life after death…
- The energy of love is the common language, no matter what one's beliefs may be.
- It is the body that weakens, gets old and dies. The spirit is always whole, strong and bright and lives forever.
- Since all beings transition, the physical body has to either wind down slowly in the natural order, or other things may happen that abruptly end a life (an acute incident or euthanasia).

This is a very important decision and the more you can educate yourself, ahead of time, preferably, the less likely you will question or judge yourself afterwards as to the validity of your decision. This can help to ease the unavoidable feelings of grief and guilt that may follow, even at a later date.

The decision to end the life by euthanasia may be unavoidable due to pain that cannot be controlled. It may also be due to the inability to care for the animal at home by reason of finance, time, ability and so on.

One concern about the commonly accepted expectation that an animal should be euthanized is that it could teach our children and ourselves that if we are afraid of something, then we end it, so we don't have to face it. If a person does decide to let their animal die naturally, albeit hospice supported, they often face incredible opposition from people who were previously very sympathetic. This unfortunate situation can be reinforced by well-meaning veterinarians, who are also trying to deal with death in an awkward human way—perhaps not understanding that death is in fact an entire process.

Animals are sentient beings, possessed of enormous wisdom, who tell their people when they are ready to go and whether they would like to be euthanized or whether they will be going naturally. Our understanding is that animals do not view euthanasia as a terrible thing and do not judge their beloved people for doing it. They just see a missed opportunity for what they know to be a sacred time ripe with many blessings and sacred wisdom. As death approaches, animals are closer to spirit than they have ever been and are so very happy to share this experience with us.

The more people are tuned in to their animal, the more they will make decisions with their animal and out of love for them, and the more they will be following the universe's divine plan. It may be that being together in love with one's beloved is the most important thing.

Of all the people I have counseled who have savored the last moments of their animals' lives, none have voiced regrets, nor do these individuals usually require ongoing counseling to resolve their feelings. They are often able to let go with love and move smoothly and meaningfully through the grieving process and the celebration of that life.

Should euthanasia be your chosen route, there is still much to consider:
- The location: in hospital or at home.
  - o Contemplate choosing an experienced at-home mobile euthanasia veterinarian.
- On occasion euthanasia will be carried out at the hospital right after diagnosis, although we would advocate to take your loved one home if possible and then make an appointment to have a veterinarian come to the house to perform the procedure if that is what has been decided after careful consideration.

Considerations and questions to be asked:
- Have the procedure fully explained to avoid surprises or questions left unanswered.
- Ask where euthanasia will be performed.
- Telephone several veterinary euthanasia services, mobile or in-hospital, to discuss your needs and ask questions, for example:
  - o What is the cost?
  - o What will be involved?
  - o What will happen afterwards?
  - o What ritual services are offered; i.e., photographs, a lock of fur or paw imprint, etc.? One can always request these too.
  - o Will the body need to be taken away immediately?
- Ensure paperwork and payment for the service is dealt with before the procedure.
- Ask if you may hold your loved one during the procedure.
- Be sure to request time alone in preparation to say goodbye.
- Be sure to ask if a sedative will be given prior to the lethal dose.
- Consider everyone who will need to say goodbye.

- Explain to children what is going to happen.

More considerations, whatever the route chosen:
- Do you wish to honor the body at home for a period of time?
- Discuss a general or private cremation or a burial.
- Consider taking the body personally to the chosen funeral home.
- Decide if you wish to be present for burial or cremation.
- An urn or casket must be chosen.
- Decide if you wish to arrange burial or cremation privately or have your veterinarian make the arrangements.
- Do you wish the ashes to be returned to your veterinarian or maybe you wish to collect them from the crematorium yourself?

Meditation, Reiki and Decision Making

Meditation:

Meditation is a precise technique for resting the mind and attaining a state of consciousness that is totally different from the normal waking state. It is the means for fathoming all the levels of ourselves and finally experiencing the center of consciousness within. Meditation is not a part of any religion; it is a science, which means that the process of meditation follows a particular order, has definite principles and produces results that can be verified.

In meditation, the mind is clear, relaxed, and inwardly focused. When you meditate, you are fully awake and alert, but your mind is not focused on the external world or on the events taking place around you. Meditation requires an inner state that is still and one-pointed so that the mind becomes silent. When the mind is silent and no longer distracts you, meditation deepens.

~*Yoga International* (www.yogainternational.com)

David Michie in his book *Buddhism for Pet Lovers* commented that

It is interesting to note the similarity between the words meditation and medication:

> They both come from the same Latin root, *medeor,*
> meaning heal, cure, remedy, assuage, comfort, amend. Whether
> we meditate or medicate, it seems that when we meditate with our
> animal loved ones, through their ease of synchronizing their minds
> with ours, we are both able to derive peace, understanding and
> healing from whatever calmness and compassion we share.
>
> ~
>
> If a person's basic state of mind is serene and calm, then it is
> possible for this inner peace to overwhelm
> a painful physical experience.
> ~*His Holiness the Dalai Lama*

Reiki and Animal Reiki

Reiki is a spiritual system cultivating compassionate intention, which in turn may bring about healing transformation. Animal Reiki is essentially meditating with your animals. The practices of Reiki help us navigate life's challenges with grace and surrender while we to learn to listen to and be present for others in a compassionate space. Offering one's self as a conduit through which energy can flow for the good of another is the single most powerful gift that one can give and receive.

During a Reiki session, animals often experience a deep state of peace as the Reiki clears imbalances, allowing for new and harmonious patterns of health and wellness to emerge. Physical contact is not a requirement for Reiki and traditionally the practitioner offers Reiki to the animal hands off. This way, the animal controls the treatment, either accepting Reiki from a distance or settling themselves against the practitioner's hands.

The practice of animal Reiki at BrightHaven began in 2004 when Kathleen Prasad began teaching monthly at the sanctuary. BrightHaven became more peaceful and harmonious, with more depth found in our relationships with our animal family and in our healing work. Reiki has proven especially invaluable during times of transition.

To be with another being with an open heart, with a listening
spirit, with a humble eye, to truly become One:
this is our experience of wisdom and compassion
as Reiki practitioners. It is not that we are doing something
to them; rather that we are sharing and being.
~Kathleen Prasad (www.animalreikisource.com)

A Few More Thoughts on Meditation, Reiki and Decision Making

Regardless of one's medical or religious views, I really feel it worth
a moment to mention the value of practicing meditation and Reiki
with our loved ones (animal and human) with regard to healing to
help support body, mind and spirit—in this instance especially the
mind, for its decision-making process.

Animals communicate using the universal language of telepathy.
All beings share this language; however, it's animals' first and
primary language. We know that telepathic communication can
be transmitted in various ways, including pictures, feelings, emotions,
physical sensations or a general "package" of knowing. And so,
when faced with difficult circumstances or decisions, please sit
quietly in meditation with your animal and assume that they can
understand you, even if you're not confident about your ability to
understand them.

Your HEART is your JUDGE, let your judge take decisions.
~Rashid Jorvee

Chapter 5: Understanding Pre- and Post-Death Grief

Think not so much of 'moving on' but of 'moving forward.'
And as you move forward, you always do so with your loved one
by your side, in your heart, within your very breath.
They are part of you now and always.
You move forward with them and continue
to engage life because of their inspiration.
~*Ashley Davis Bush*

Despite receiving a terminal diagnosis, we may naturally hold on to the hope that new and healthier life may be right around the corner, and for some it will be, but others will follow the progression towards the end of life.

Pre-Death or Anticipatory Grief

If someone is facing a difficult time, one of the kindest
things you can do for him or her is to say,
"I'm going to love you through this."
~*Molly Friedenfeld*

Regardless of our hopes and dreams, we have learned that our grieving process actually begins when we are told that the end of this life may be sooner than expected. Animals clearly know it and, in our experience, show no fear. We humans often cannot help but hold that fear of death in our hearts.

The last few months of life are a special time of preparation and anticipation, when everyone is beginning to accept that death is just around the corner. Many animals have shown us that this is the time to begin to step into acceptance of what is and to let go of fears surrounding the future.

Before death has occurred may seem a strange place for us to begin a conversation about grieving, but this is not so, as grieving can occur either before or after death, or both. The typical human pattern of death followed by the grieving process is one we have learned to reverse at BrightHaven, as animals have shown us their way. By following the wisdom of animals we've learned to begin grieving and saying our goodbyes as soon as we accept death to be inevitable. We feel truly blessed to be able to spend this extraordinary time with our loved ones, in togetherness before they leave.

A child's grieving process is affected by age and maturity. We all grieve, no matter our age, but our understanding of this normal life experience varies with age. In our BrightHaven experience we have found that children like to talk and learn about what is going on, and often step into acceptance with grace and ease, grieving with the animals before they die.

> Don't cry because it's over,
> Smile because it happened.
> *~Dr. Seuss*

It's a time to discuss shared experiences and fond memories:
- We talk about how much we love them and how much we will miss their physical presence.
- We cry together.
- We laugh together, and we share everything.
- We accept that death is coming and prepare for the event together.

There is nothing more sacred than to care for a beloved friend during his or her final time with us on earth. The bond created during these profound moments is one never to be forgotten. We share this precious time together in love, knowing that we will always be together in spirit and will one day meet again.

In the hours, days and sometimes weeks before death becomes final, we have witnessed many groups of animals gathering together to share love and celebrate the life of one of their own who was dying. Observing the course of their experience, we realized that grief no longer existed for these animal "nurses" after death had taken place. Sometimes animals remain with the dead body for a period of time but some will return quickly to normal life, behavior and appetite, very often choosing new places to sleep or play. The atmosphere is one of joy, honor and celebration.

And so, in the course of our education in the final stages of life, we came to realize that our grief had very often actually passed by the time death occurred.

> How lucky I am to have something that makes
> saying goodbye so hard.
> ~*A.A. Milne*, Winnie-the-Pooh

Grief After Death

> What we have once enjoyed we can never lose.
> All that we love deeply becomes a part of us.
> ~*Helen Keller*

It's important to know that there's no right way to grieve, and certainly no timetable.

Everyone mourns in his or her own way, and in his or her own time. Don't let anyone tell you otherwise!

Very often, once the honoring period is over, grief may come flooding in again. You may be experiencing a few welcome moments of serenity when you are suddenly blindsided and sucked into a new, forceful vortex of sorrow.

Grief, like all emotions, is energy in motion that needs to be felt and then released. This awareness can help one cope with the emotional roller coaster ride. There is nothing to fear from emotions!

Grief is unique to every individual:
There are, however, some typical responses to grief and loss that may be encountered.

- Revisiting
    - o Often the grieving heart relentlessly revisits the final weeks, days, hours and minutes of a loved one's life.
- Review
    - o Perhaps this futile process of ceaseless review helps one to continue to hold on to the departed—if it's still going on in your mind, then it's not over.
- Denial
    - o Numbness, disorientation, feeling overwhelmed; a feeling of being in a trance or simply just not present, or that life is surreal. One is in a state of shock, but these feelings will slowly help one to come to terms with the loss.
- Investigation
    - o Perhaps it's a painful search for clues as to how the outcome to such a horrible story could somehow be rewritten.
- Regrets
    - o What wasn't said or done, what shouldn't have been said or done…
- Blame and anger
    - o A typical grief response is to place blame. On others, including doctors and anyone else who tried to improve the situation but obviously failed, because the loved one still died.
    - o Anger may also be felt towards your deceased animal. This is all about your pain and the depth of your love.
- Helplessness
    - o An overpowering sense of helplessness about the situation can also cause painful self-blame.
- Bargaining
    - o Guilt often accompanies bargaining and is basically our way of transferring the deep pain of the loss. Along with this come the "what if" questions.
- Depression
    - o It's important to understand that after the loss of a loved one, depression is a perfectly normal emotional response. During this stage, you will likely feel as though you are in a fog of sadness, sometimes worsened by those who are not animal lovers or who simply do not understand your grief.

- Acceptance
    - o There comes a time when you can accept life now without your loved one. That doesn't mean they are forgotten, moved aside or even that you are okay with everything, merely that you have reached a point where you can start to move forward in daily life.

There are some things to be done that may help:
- Talk
    - o It can be very helpful to talk with a grief counselor to help you to work through your feelings.
- Cry
    - o Crying helps. Tears are for cleansing and releasing.
- Breathe
    - o Remember that emotions are connected to breathing patterns. Practice taking long, slow and deep breaths and remember to exhale!
- Use positive affirmations. Here are two that I love:
    - o This too shall pass.
    - o Today I focus on loving myself, and gratitude and trust in the process.

They do tell us when it's time.
And that's the origin of the pain,
exquisitely painful;
also, a relief.
No more pain for the afflicted one.
Pain and joy and memory, all tied up together.

~Dian Hardy

Sooner or later one must return to daily life and go back to work, do the grocery shopping, mix with family and friends and so on. This can prove very difficult, as many people feel very uncomfortable encountering the raw emotion of grief in others and deal with it in an awkward, even dismissive way. Sometimes grief is even viewed as a sign of weakness. All this can result in one's feeling more isolated in a fog of sorrow with feelings of guilt and depression exacerbated.

If on the other hand one tries to act normal and hide grief from others one might be viewed sometimes as "doing well" or "being strong." This is often an incorrect assessment and grief held in check is not a very healthy way to deal with emotions. It can sometimes return later in life quite unexpectedly and therefore it is beneficial, as well as healing, to mourn outwardly. Again, it is important to have someone—family, a friend or a support group—with whom to share your feelings.

Remember, there is no right way to grieve, and no timetable.

> When you are sorrowful look again in your heart,
> and you shall see that in truth you are weeping
> for that which has been your delight.
> *~Kahlil Gibran*

Chapter 6: Lessons from Animals

Here are just a few of the important lessons I have learned from animals.

- Love really IS the most important thing.
- Remember to smile—it's contagious!
- Living in the present moment is key.
- Animals speak our language as well as their own—be careful to share conversations.
- Healthy living = gentle dying.
- Acceptance of what "is" is key—as well as being open to change…hmm.
- Caring is more about "being" than "doing."
- The term "dying" can sit in one's mind if allowed but we really are only ALIVE or DEAD. Therefore, during a terminal illness, one should focus on life and not death.
- It really is never over until it's over.
- Embracing death as a natural part of life = full living.
- Animals show no apparent fear of death.
- Dying is a slow, gradual process, an orderly progression designed by Mother Nature.
- Dying does not always look the same. It's as unique as each individual.
- Dying is not a failed medical event.
- Dying is part of living.
- It's all about living well through the last breath!
- There is light after life.

There is only one happiness in life, to love and be loved.
~George Sand

Now I would like to share a few short, inspirational and true stories to inspire belief that dreams may come true, there may be more to life, miracles can happen and there may well be an afterlife.

Hazel

They said she could not survive out of the oxygen tank. Her care-taker still decided to take her home to die. Hazel did not have an acute episode but her breathing adjusted and she had acupuncture treatment and continued to wind down slowly as nature intended, to die peacefully in her loved one's arms some weeks later.

Mack

Hypertrophic cardiomyopathy was diagnosed, and his chest tapped several times to remove fluid for more comfort. Euthanasia was insisted upon by the concerned veterinarian, but Mack was taken home to die. Nine months later he continued to do well with loving, holistic and supportive care.

Olivia

Olivia at 13 years was a four-pound feline athlete mainly to be found teetering on top of our highest doors or pot shelves that no one else could reach. Her eyes and fur shone with good health and joi de vivre and she was adored by all. In 2004 I was diagnosed with a large mass in my chest and refused invasive action, preferring to follow Wayne Dyer's vision of the power of intention. Several months later Olivia suddenly could not jump to her high places or even low ones and became quiet. A mobile ultrasound specialist discovered a huge mass in her chest. She died easily and very quickly 3 days later. It was a long time afterwards that I made the obvious connection...

Furbee

Furbee was a brain-damaged kitten, having been tossed from a car window. He was not expected to live, but did, and the severe seizures he had regularly for 14 years did not seem to affect his overall health at all. He had as many as 19 seizures on one difficult day. We learned how to best care for and communicate with him and he did well until going into renal failure towards the end of life. Everyone wondered what his death would be like and if he would seizure badly through the process. During the last weeks of his life he had not one seizure and died easily and peacefully.

Johnnie

Johnnie was a truly gifted healer who spent his early years in love with, and offering healing to, many animals. After his last great love, Vancouver, died, Johnnie turned his attention to healing the human heart.

At Reiki seminars Johnnie welcomed everyone before he selected his person. He then spread himself across the chosen individual's heart. Time and time again, Johnnie's loving presence produced streams of tears of release from those with aching hearts: some who had lost loved ones and been unable to cry, others who were suffering illness or some other emotional life event. Everyone felt better afterwards, ready again to face life in a new way. Johnnie suffered chronic illness of his own later in life, most notably that of his own heart, which manifested about the same time he started to heal others' hearts...

Mariah

In 1995, Mariah at 26 became my own first natural dying experience. She wound down slowly and easily over a period of months, as her appetite and will to live gradually diminished. Eventually she became wobbly of gait, could no longer eat or drink and was clearly dying. I made the decision to euthanize her but could not leave the sanctuary that day to take her to the vet as I was alone. I spent the afternoon sitting with Mariah under the branches of a spreading oak tree in our garden, her lying relaxed and breathing softly and slowly. And me? I was very busy trying not to be filled with fear and panic and waiting for something awful to happen.

What happened was that Mariah eventually passed away very peacefully in my arms with only a gentle sigh. At the time I blamed myself for allowing her to suffer and die that way. Much later I realized that my own fear, pain, heartache and suffering had masked the actual beauty of her death.

King Tut

King Tut had a large squamous cell tumor in his throat. and we wondered if we might have to intervene at the end of his life. We expected him to be unable to breathe. and used our imagination to understand what the tumor was doing... As it turned out, he drooled quite a lot, ate as best he could for as long as he felt the need. His breathing didn't change until it slowed at the very end and he died holding my hands with his paws, very present and very easily.

Nicki and the Dove

Several years ago, our horse Nicki approached the end of her life and we chose to support her with hospice care around the clock in the pasture. NOT an easy thing. She was treated integratively and wound down slowly. It was hard to watch a large being incapacitated and we had the euthanasia discussion daily with our team. Then the rains came, and the pasture became waterlogged. We dragged her to dryer ground but realized the water would soon reach her. The decision was finally and regretfully made to euthanize in the morning and her vet was called. Richard and I spent that last night cuddling her and explaining what would happen. At 6:30 in the morning a dove appeared on the ground at Nicki's head. They looked at each other for what seemed an interminable time and then Nicki swung her huge head around to stare hard into Richard's eyes. She then turned back—the dove flew westwards, and Nicki's legs began to gallop, before she left her body behind.

Ellie

Ellie was an elderly, very beautiful feline lady, approximately 17, who came from a Los Angeles animal shelter to live with us after her euthanasia recommendation. She had a squamous cell carcinoma on one eyelid and a huge bladder tumor that restricted and sometimes stopped her urinary flow badly. The bladder mass also caused a lot of inflammation. which in turn also caused daily bleeding spells and urinary troubles.

After searching in vain for surgical options Ellie was simply cared for following the BrightHaven Menu for Healing (www.brighthaven.org/animal-wellbeing-menu-healing/) including classical veterinary homeopathy courtesy of Dr. Jeff Levy (www.homeovet.net/), and cannabis tinctures from King Harvest (www.kingharvest.org/). Life for Ellie was about living in the moment from day to day—a tough lesson for us to follow, but we had no choice! Ellie's eye and bladder tumors remained mostly quiet and her morning bleeding episodes finally stopped completely, and she then experienced a little better urine flow.

The best part? Ellie loved her life, everyone in it and demonstrated that with THE loudest purr when spoken to! Ellie wound down slowly and gracefully to die almost two years after her arrival. Her death was all we could have wished for, and as peaceful, slow and dignified as she deserved.

Many days of my own, wasted in worry and fear, stand out clearly in hindsight and in contrast to her wisdom.

Alfie

Alfie was the cutest little happy dog who like many others seemed to lose his reason towards the end of his life. Was this dementia? Was he in pain? What could we do? Our questions were endless. All the while Alfie sank deeper into his private place of sleeping, interspersed with long periods of barking, wailing or howling...The days passed, and the suffering mounted. Ours, for sure. His? We knew not. He could not eat on his own or do anything on his own, even stand up. Finally, we made the decision to euthanize him and our veterinarian kindly came to the sanctuary. We gathered around. In his final moments Alfie seemed suddenly clear and gazed at us knowingly—but too late. The deed was done, and we were again filled with worries and fear...

Copy

Dee Days Copy was strong of body, mind and spirit until he was not. Passionate and powerful quarter horses do not give up that easily, though, and so the journey began...until the day he could no longer walk, and we knew we should make a final choice. With the telephone call made and nothing to do but sit together in the pasture, we spent our time in memories and stories of his past adventures on the trails with Richard. I explained to him carefully what was going to happen, and he appeared to listen intently. We suggested he should leave of his own accord, if that was possible. He did not, of course, but then, as our veterinarian's truck drew into the drive Copy looked deeply at us both, gave a huge sigh and, in that moment, died.

Alexi and Woodstock

Two cats who could not have been more different! Alexi was a frail, tiny, rounded Siamese with no voice and Woodstock, a long-legged scruffy tabby with a huge growl. Both were nearing the end of life and this was the day of Woodstock's passing—a gentle and slow journey for him. Alexi, on the other hand was not ready but had a very painful, abscessed tooth that needed removal. What to do? Would—could—he even survive a surgery? What other option was there?

The decision was finally made, and Woodstock finally died very easily, peacefully and naturally in my arms just moments before I had to leave with Alexi for the hospital...

Survive the surgery he did and after coming home Alexi slept soundly in his cubby for many hours. Finally he awoke, gazed dreamily at me for several seconds and then opening his dainty little mouth out came that very familiar, well-loved and huge growly meow of you-know-who...!

> You have to leave the city of your comfort
> and go into the wilderness of your intuition.
> What you'll discover will be wonderful.
> What you'll discover is yourself.
> ~*Alan Alda*

Conclusion

Please accept my sincere appreciation for reading *Follow Your Heart: Navigating a Terminal Diagnosis*. I hope you found it informative, helpful and hopefully even inspiring, during what must perhaps be one of the most difficult and challenging times one ever has to face for and with a loved one.

My heart goes out to you If you are struggling with thoughts and decisions as to the way forward. Having cared for more than 600 animals during the last chapters of their lives for 30 years I can honestly say that I have learned more than I can ever say about the circle of life and love.

So many wise and wonderful animals have taught me about following my heart, living in the moment, letting go of my fears, remembering the wisdom of animals, sharing my heart with them and above all realizing that I can do no more than my best—with so much love.

Hope may be an important part of this journey. However, we should remember that hope looks to the future, and being present in the moment and therefore available now is a tremendous help to everyone concerned, including yourself.

Dying is a part of living, not a mistake or some type of punish-ment. I encourage you to learn more about dying and death as knowledge greatly reduces fear. I've found that when one isn't afraid of these inevitable occurrences, one is able to live more fully. And this is the perfect place to remind you, my dear reader, that we are all fully alive until we are not.

Perhaps mostly I have learned that there really is no greater gift than to be fully present with our loved ones during the last chapter of their lives, to share love with them, to make decisions together and not in fear, and to do so with courage and grace.

With my love, blessings and gratitude,

Gail Pope

President & Founder, BrightHaven

Autumn is a second spring
when every leaf is a flower.
~Albert Camus

Navigation by the Heart

Today I woke up and it was different from yesterday.

My fears and concerns are fading away.
My energy is focused not on the past, but on the now.

I'm navigating all my thoughts on how to better help you,
my sunshine.
My heart hurts and I feel so helpless watching you lying in my arms.
Your eyes full of life remind me there's so much that still can be done.

Can I handle it all, I ask myself so many times?
I can't lose hope as I'm reminded by you every day and every night
of the beautiful gift of life we have.

In the middle of confusion and despair, you've shown me in so
many ways to never give up.
There's always hope, there's always a way.
There is always a chance to make this journey better for both of us.
You've truly shown me the meaning of life is to live in the moment
and not in the past.

Our boats may sail from different docks, but our destination
will be the same, as we navigate by the compass of love and life

This poem is dedicated to all those whom I have loved, who brought
light to my life and showed me the true meaning of unconditional love.

By Blanca Walker
BrightHaven Social Media Specialist & Graphic Artist
BrightHaven Animal Care Specialist 2004-2018

Suggested Resources

*   Website: www.brighthaven.org
*   Consultations with Gail Pope, President and Founder: www.brighthaven.org/products-and-services/consultations/
*   Online education program: www.brighthaven.org/education/
*   Books on Amazon by Gail Pope, President and Founder: https://amzn.to/1Ky7jnu
*   Book on Amazon by Carol Howe Hulse, Education Program Specialist: https://amzn.to/2coRncm

If you purchase a book via https://smile.amazon.com/ and select BrightHaven as your favorite charitable organization, Amazon will donate a percentage of the sale price to BrightHaven.

Hospice Websites
*   International Association of Animal Hospice and Palliative Care {IAAHPC): www.iaahpc.org
*   International Association of Animal Hospice and Palliative Care Guidelines: www.iaahpc.org/resources-and-support/practice-guidelines.html
*   National Hospice and Palliative Care Organization: www. nhpco.org
*   Spirits in Transition: www.spiritsintransition.org
*   The Hospice Foundation of America: www.hospicefounda-tion.org
*   The Nikki Hospice Foundation: www.pethospice.org

Suggested Resources to Obtain Help and Guidance Regarding Animal Hospice
*   BrightHaven Center for Animal Rescue, Hospice and Holistic Education: www.brighthaven.org
*   Hospice and Palliative Care: The International Association for Animal Hospice and Palliative Care: https://iaahpc.org/for-the-professional/faq.html

- Spirits in Transition: www.spiritsintransition.org
- The Nikki Hospice Foundation: www.pethospice.org
- The Animal Hospice Certificate: www.brighthaven.org/animal-hospice-care-certificate/
- The Quality of Dying Checklist: www.brighthaven.org/quality-dying-checklist/
- GRACE* Animal Hospice: www.graceanimalhospice.org/
  - o Animal hospice defined: www.graceanimalhospice.org/animal-hospice-defined/
  - o Foundational principles of animal hospice: www.graceanimalhospice.org/foundational-principles-of-hospice/

* GRACE is a collaborative effort between BrightHaven, Spirits in Transition and The Nikki Hospice Foundation.

Definitions

- Conventional Medicine: www.webmd.com/cancer/qa/what-is-conventional-medicine
- Holistic Medicine: www.webmd.com/balance/guide/what-is-holistic-medicine#1
- Integrative Medicine: www.webmd.com/cancer/holistic-treatment-17/integrative-medicine
- Hospice and Palliative Care: The International Association for Animal Hospice and Palliative Care: www.iaahpc.org/for-the-professional/faq.html
- Animal Hospice defined—GRACE Animal Hospice: www.graceanimalhospice.org/animal-hospice-defined/
- Foundational principles of animal hospice— GRACE Animal Hospice: www.graceanimalhospice.org/foundational-principles-of-hospice/

Classical Veterinary Homeopaths (all BrightHaven volunteers)

Christine Barret DVM
530 367-3672

Diana Bochenski DVM, CVH
805 688-2334

Buellton Veterinary Clinic

Pat Bradley DVM, LPC
501 329-7727
www.drpatbradley.com

Christina Chambreau DVM
410 771-4968
www.christinachambreau.com, www.holisticactions.com

Jeff Feinman BA, DVM, CVH
203 222-7979
www.homevet.com, www.holisticactions.com

Jeff Levy DVM, PCH
413 268-3000
www.homeovet.net

Laurie Lofton DVM, CVH
401 568-4154

Francie Rubin DVM, CVH
215 379-1677
Rockledge Veterinary Clinic
www.rockledgevet.com/about/veterinarians-staff-l-rubin-vmd/73/

Adriana Sagrera DVM, CVH
504 834-2023
www.drsagrera.com

Michele Yasson DVM
845 338-3300
www.holvet.net

Animal Telepath and Medical Intuitive
July Berrin
+44 7583 694993

www.thetemplecat.uno

Richard Bach
Avid aviator and author, touching on themes of flight and enlight-
enment
        Works include *Jonathan Livingston Seagull*; *Illusions*

Karen Whitley Bell RN
        Works include *Living at the End of Life*: *A Hospice Nurse
Addresses the Most Common Questions*

Gregg Braden
Scientist, visionary & scholar
        Works include *The Divine Matrix*

Richard F. Groves
Executive Director at Sacred Art of Living Center
        Works include *The American Book of Living and Dying*

Thích Nhất Hạnh
Vietnamese Buddhist monk, teacher, author, poet and peace activist
        Works include *Being Peace*; *Moments of Mindfulness*

Wendy Hayhurst
Certified Soul Midwife
        Works include *Coming for to Carry Me Home*

Barbara Karnes RN
End-of-life nurse and hospice educator
        Works include *Gone from my Sight*

Dr. Konstantin G. Korotkov
Russian biophysicist, inventor, and pioneer of the scientific field
called electrophotonics; invented the Gas Discharge Visualization,
or GDV, technique by which the energy fields emanating from
humans may be viewed in real time

Works include *Light after Life*

Elizabeth Kübler-Ross
Pioneer in near-death studies and celebrated author
        Works include *On Death and Dying*

Bruce Lipton
An internationally recognized leader in bridging soul and spirit
        Works include *The Biology of Belief*

David Michie Ph.D.
Author
        Works include *The Dalai Lama's Cat* series of novels, as well as non-fiction titles including *Why Mindfulness is Better than Chocolate; Hurry Up and Meditate; Buddhism for Busy People; Buddhism for Pet Lovers*

Michael Newton Ph.D.
Author & Founder of The Newton Institute for life Between Lives
        Works include *Destiny of Souls; Memories of the Afterlife*

M. Scott Peck
        Works include *Denial of the Soul: Spiritual and Medical Perspectives on Euthanasia and Mortality*

Kathleen Prasad
Animal Reiki educator
        Works include *The Animal Reiki Handbook; Reiki for Dogs*

Sogyal Rinpoche
A Tibetan Dzogchen lama of the Nyingma tradition; the founder and spiritual director of Rigpa
        Works include *The Tibetan Book of Living and Dying*

Amir Shanan, Jessica Pierce and Tamara Shearer, Editors
Hospice and Palliative Care for Companion Animals: Principles and Practice, Chapter 22: "Comfort Care during Active Dying," Gail

Pope and Amir Shanan

Brian L. Weiss M.D.
Author, psychiatrist and hypnotherapist who specializes in past life regression
        Works include *Many Lives, Many Masters*

Paramahansa Yogananda
Indian yogi
        Works include *Autobiography of a Yogi*

My Mentors
Christine Barrett DVM
530 367-3672

Douglas Coward DVM
Animal and Bird Clinic of Mission Viejo
http://abcofmv.vetstreet.com/our_staff.html

Jeff Levy DVM, PCH
Classical Veterinary Homeopathy
413 268-3000
www.homeovet.net/

Kathleen Prasad
Animal Reiki Source
415 420-9783
www.animalreikisource.com/about/kathleen-prasad/

Amir Shanan DVM, CHPV
Compassionate Veterinary Hospice
773 244-1045
www.pethospicechicago.com/about/dr-amir-shanan-dvm

        Adopt the pace of nature: her secret is patience.
                                ~*Ralph Waldo Emerson*

Notes

To order more copies visit www.amazon.com. If you purchase via
smile.amazon.com and select BrightHaven as your favorite charitable organization, Amazon will donate a percentage of the purchase price to BrightHaven!

For information please contact:

BrightHaven Inc

44489 Town Center Way,
Ste D 487
Palm Desert, CA92260

www.ingramcontent.com/pod-product-compliance
Lightning Source LLC
Chambersburg PA
CBHW061729250726
48657CB00002B/839